MASTERMIND MAZES

Written and illustrated by

PATRICK MERRELL

Troll

Caitlin | Isabel
Kathy + Woody
Doug
Greg + Ann
Dedicated to

Note to readers: All the material in this book is true, with the following exceptions:
•The Mayztec never existed •There is a Trans-Siberian Railroad, but its route is much simpler •There is no Great Siberian Shaft, no Minotaur Miniature Golf Course, no Hatun Owango, and no Sven Zeitfleugen. Sara Bellum and Sir Rebral are, however, real cartoon characters.

Look for these other Troll maze books by Patrick Merrell:
MAZE★MANIA
MONSTER MAZES

Welcome to Mastermind Headquarters. I am Sara Bellum, and this is my chief maze tester, Sir Rebral. Behind these walls are some of the toughest, most tantalizingly tangled tests of trail-twisting treachery known to man, woman, boy, girl, dog, cat, sea slug, or ungulated ruminant (you probably call them cows).

I have collected these mazes from around the world, selecting only those that are truly worthy of the title Mastermind Maze. You're probably thinking you could solve these mazes. Forget it! Even Sir Rebral has trouble with them, and just look at the size of his enormously large and brainy head.

Of course, if you'd still like to try, you're more than welcome. It's just that I wouldn't get my hopes up too much....

Mazes have been rated as follows:

M Mastermind

MM Major Mastermind

MMM MonuMental Mastermind

1 MAIZE MAZE

Maize, or common corn, was an important food for many of the ancient Mexican tribes. The Aztecs even prayed to a Maize god. The stone carving shown below is one I discovered while down in Mexico. It shows a field of maize that has been planted in the shape of, well, a maze. Beginning at "Start," can you find a path between the rows of maize to the shining sun? **M**

'Ears an easy one

Start

End

2 'TEC TREK

There have been many great Mexican civilizations. The Maya and the Aztec are two of the most famous. Less well known is a small tribe that resulted from a mix of these two empires. That tribe was known as the Mayztec.

The Mayztec lived on the western shores of Central America around A.D. 1300 to 1400. They had many treasures, so as a defense, they built the legendary temple of Ixocali. The temple's twisted jumble of paths and staircases was so difficult to get through that invading armies would often just give up.

I bought this scale model of Ixocali at a small stand on the outskirts of Mazatlan, Mexico. Starting at the large stairway in the lower right, can you find the way up to the treasure room at the top?

Next

Ooohh

MM

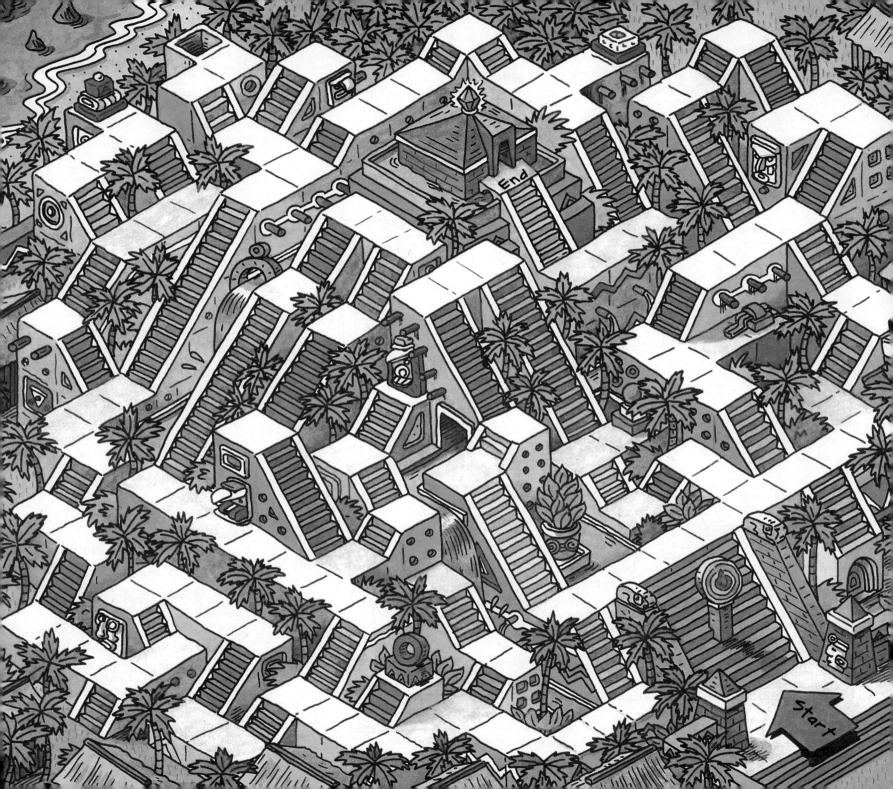

3 RAIL TRAIL

Getting around in Siberia can be pretty difficult. One way is by train, using the Trans-Siberian Railroad. That's the way I took when I was there. The train map I used is shown below. Starting from Moscow, can you figure out which set of railroad tracks my train took to get me to Irkutsk? **M**

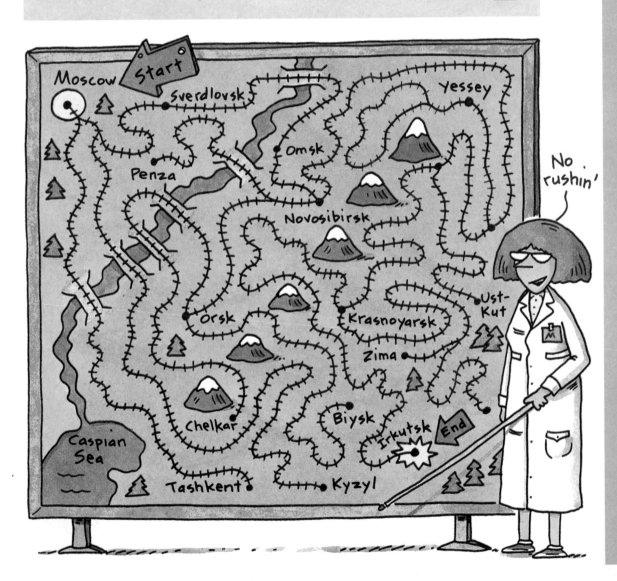

4 IN A HOLE

Russia is one of the largest producers of gold, iron, and coal in the world. This also makes it one of the largest producers of holes in the world. Very deep holes. With lots of tunnels.

Looking for a way to use these leftover holes, the Siberian government came up with an idea. What if they were to link several mineshafts together and offer tours? The result was the Great Siberian Shaft.

When I was in the area several years ago, I made a detour to see the Great Siberian Shaft, and let me tell you, it lived up to its billing. On the next page, you will see a map of the underground park.

Beginning at the entrance in the upper right, can you find the way a tour guide would take a group through these mineshafts? You can ride an elevator up or down, stopping at any tunnel it passes.

Hot dig-gety!

MM

I just installed a spotlight for one of our new exhibits. As you can see, it has created quite a jumble of extension cords on the floor. Starting at the outlet in the floor, can you figure out which path of cords leads to the spotlight? **M**

Gotta be bright for this one.

6 **BOARD YET?**

Really good mazes can sometimes be found in the most unlikely places. Take the maze on the next page. It is actually a circuit board from inside an old television set.

I discovered it while strolling through a used-electronics store on Canal Street in New York City. To tell you the truth, it wasn't until I got it home that I realized just what I had—two new Mastermind Mazes.

Following the red traces (the red lines) on this circuit board, can you get from "Start" to the main processor? Following the green traces, can you get from the main processor back to "Start"?

When your route brings you to one of the large rectangles (these are the chips and connectors), you may exit that rectangle by following any *same-colored* trace that leads out of it.

Keep on plugging.

MM

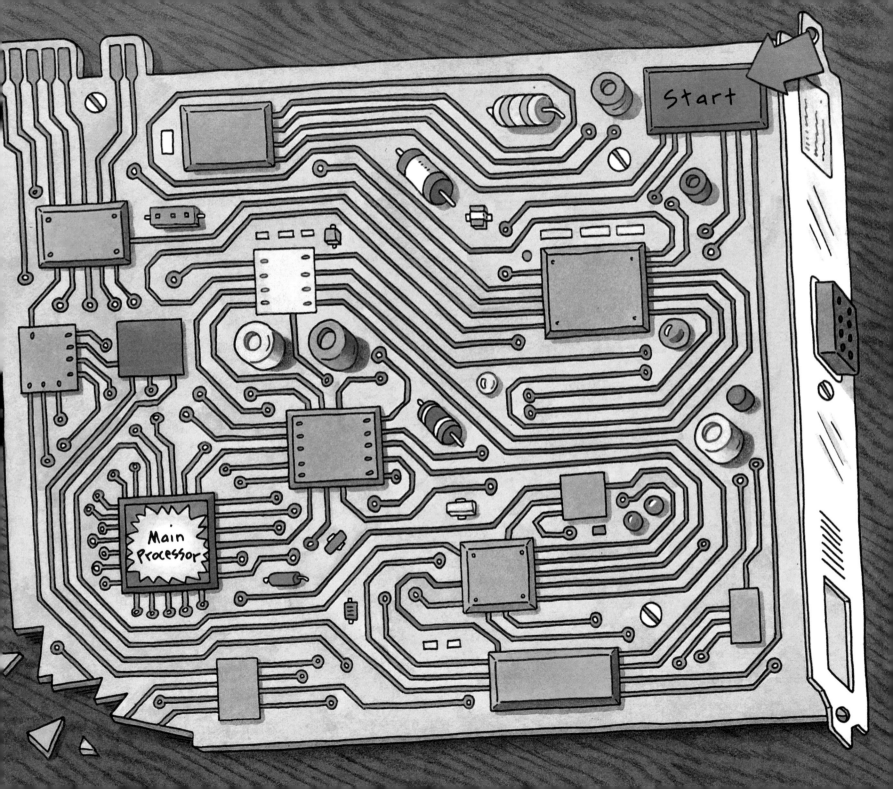

7 IT'S ALL GREEK TO ME

The grid below contains letters from the Greek alphabet. You don't have to know which is which. All you have to do is try to get from "A" (alpha) in the upper left to "Ω" (omega) in the lower right. Here's how it works:

1. Start with "A." Find *any* other square with an "A" in it and move to that square.
2. Pick the other letter from the square you are now in.
3. Move to any other square with that letter in it.
4. Keep picking and moving until you get to "Ω."

8 MINOTAUR GOLF

On a trip to Crete, a Greek island in the Mediterranean Sea, I came across this maze. It is actually the eighteenth hole from the Minotaur Miniature Golf Course.

The Minotaur was a creature in ancient Greek mythology with the head of a bull and the body of a man. King Minos of Crete put the Minotaur in the Labyrinth, a maze from which there was no escape.

This golf hole is a labyrinth like the one King Minos used. The only difference is, you have to try to get into the middle of it—using a putter and golf ball.

Can you figure out which tee to use so your golf ball will end up in the Minotaur's hole in the middle?

You'll need a lot of drive to get through this.

9 GO GET 'EM

Go is a game that has been played in Japan for centuries. Players put small black or white pieces on a large board, trying to gain the most territory. Below, we have used a Go board in a different way. We have covered the board with the black and white pieces to create a maze. Can you figure out which color, black or white, has a continuous line of pieces that goes all the way from the left side of the board to the right? **MM**

10 TILT!

In Japan, they play another popular game called Pachinko. It`s kind of like a pinball game that's been put up on its end. A player shoots small steel balls up to the top, trying to get them to come down in the highest scoring spots at the bottom.

The Pachinko game on the next page is one I found in the Ginza district of Tokyo, Japan. This particular game is especially challenging because there is only one way for the balls to end up in the highest scoring spot at the bottom (the 500 box). There is also only one way to end up in the next highest scoring spot (the 100 box). There are many ways to end up in the other boxes.

Care to try your luck? After the ball zooms to the top, pick a path down through the pins to see how you score. (Only one rule: you have to follow the laws of gravity—no going back up!)

Bing Bing Bing

MMM

Start

End

11 VINE LINE

Several months ago, I received a letter from a Chilean melon farmer about an unusual melon vine he had discovered growing on his *hacienda* (ranch). I went down there to check it out and found myself looking at what has now become a popular exhibit at Mastermind Headquarters—the world's only melon-vine maze.

You will see the vine displayed on the page to the left. Starting at the spot where the plant grows out of the soil, can you find a path through the long, twisting vine to the melon at the end?

EXTRA CREDIT

(There is something unusual about the correct route through this maze. Can you figure out what it is?)

creepy

MMM

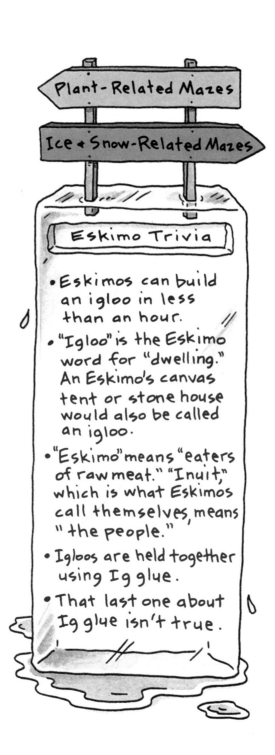

Plant-Related Mazes

Ice & Snow-Related Mazes

Eskimo Trivia

- Eskimos can build an igloo in less than an hour.
- "Igloo" is the Eskimo word for "dwelling." An Eskimo's canvas tent or stone house would also be called an igloo.
- "Eskimo" means "eaters of raw meat." "Inuit," which is what Eskimos call themselves, means "the people."
- Igloos are held together using Ig glue.
- That last one about Ig glue isn't true.

12 I SEE

When I was in Greenland one year, I stumbled across a small festival put together by the local Eskimos. It included an ice-sculpting contest, a dogsled race, and lots of *mattak*, an Eskimo dish of fermented narwhal skin and blubber. The highlight of the event, though, was a large igloo maze. I was so impressed with it that I had a picture made. You will see it displayed on the next two pages.

Half of this maze goes above ground, half of it underground. Each igloo in the maze has a number carved in its side. Igloos with the same number are connected by an underground tunnel. Some of the igloos are also connected by paths. By following the trail of paths and tunnels, can you find your way from the starting sign on the left-hand page to Rock Island on the right-hand page?

Cool

MM

Next page

13 WATER WAY TO GO

Coral reefs can sometimes be made up of lots of smaller reefs. On the map below, you will notice a complex group of coral reefs just off the shore of a large island.

Starting from the boat at sea, can you find a way to row the boat through the openings in the reef so it will end up at the small dock on the island? **M**

Kid to librarian: where would I find coral?

Librarian: Under C or undersea.

Start

End

14 GOOD G-REEF

The maze on the next page is a brain coral. It came from a trip I made to the Great Barrier Reef, just off the northeastern coast of Australia.

The Great Barrier Reef is the largest coral formation in the world, stretching for more than 1,200 miles (1,930 km). Each piece of coral in the reef is actually a colony of tiny animals, called coral polyps, living together in a limestone structure they have built.

Coral comes in many different sizes and shapes. In a brain coral, the polyps live side by side between high walls of limestone. As you can see, this can create a complicated structure.

In the brain coral shown here, there are actually two mazes. One goes along the top of the brain coral's ridges. The other goes between the ridges, where the polyps live. Can you figure out both routes from "Start" to "End"?

top route: **M**   polyp route: **M M M**

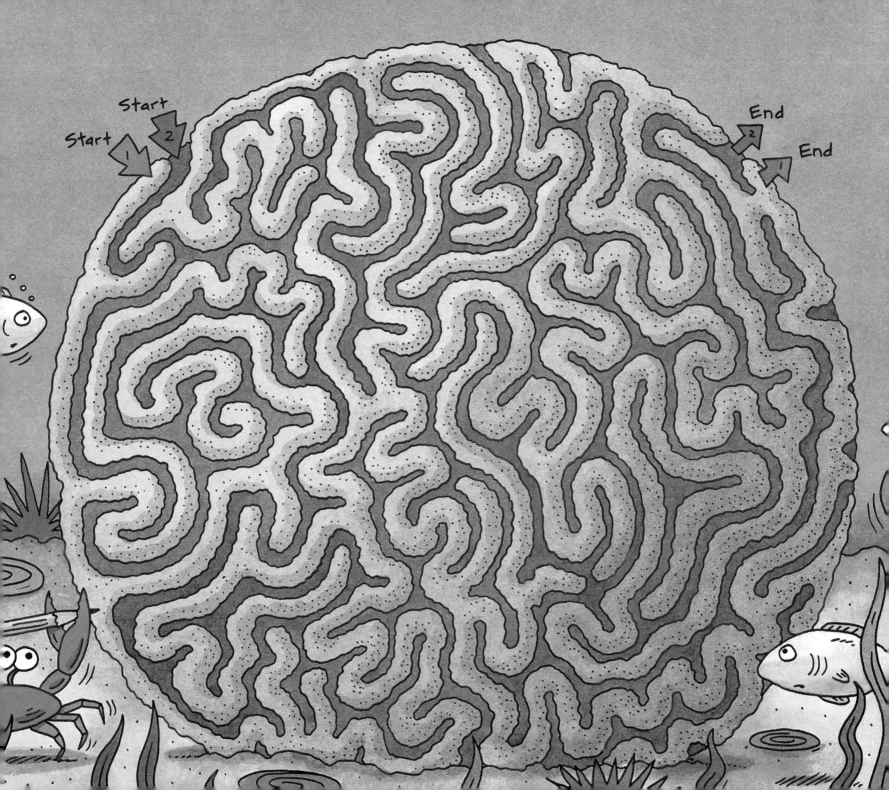

FOLLOW THE BOUNCING BALL

This lumpy ball bounces in odd directions. Starting at "A," can you find which path this bouncing ball followed to end up at the spot marked "B"? **MM**

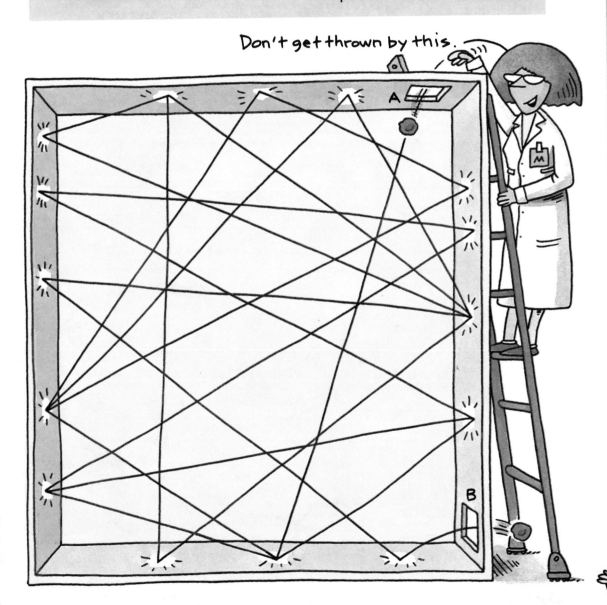

Don't get thrown by this.

HAVE A BALL

A child's toy. A simple sounding thing, but not when it's one made by Hatun Owango.

Hatun lives in a small village at the edge of the Kalahari Desert in southern Africa. During the day, Hatun can usually be found under the shade of his favorite thorn tree, carving one of the intricate wooden toys he is famous for. He has named these toys Owangos.

To play an Owango, one tries to tilt it so that a marble at the top will follow the right path and land in the "pool of luck" at the bottom. Since there are many tracks in an Owango, and only one route leads to the "pool of luck," this can be difficult to do.

Starting at the top, can you find the lucky path through this Owango? (Marbles can roll uphill.)

I can't do this one. I've lost all my marbles.

MM

17 ROLL ON

The quilt below has a dice pattern on it that makes an interesting maze. It's a little tricky, but here's how it works:

1. Each die has 3 faces outlined with a heavy black line.

2. You can move freely from one face on a die to any other face on that same die.

3. You can move from one die to another die—but only where the touching faces have the same number showing. Can you solve the maze? **MM**

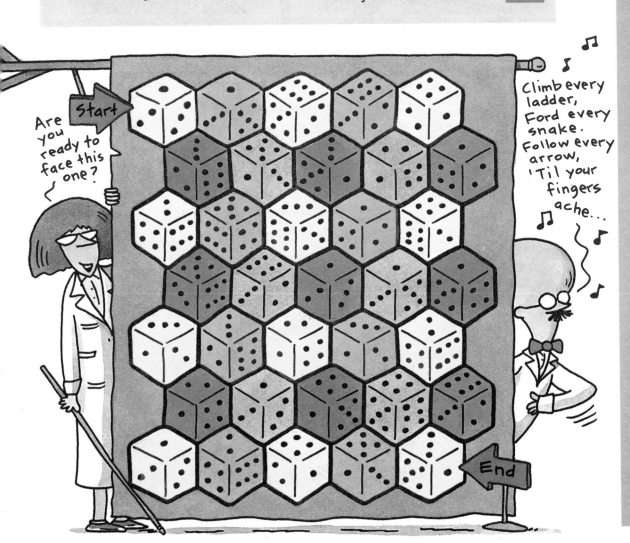

18 NO DICE

The game of Snakes and Ladders (known better as Chutes and Ladders) originally came from an Indian game called Moksha-Patamu. The ladders were rewards for good behavior; the snakes were penalties for bad behavior.

Not too long ago, when I was in the city of Nagpur, India, I came across an old game of Snakes and Ladders. As I studied the board, I made a startling discovery—hidden in it was a clever maze. Using the following instructions, can you solve it?

No dice are needed—move along the game board as you would any maze. Beginnning at "Start," move from square to square in the direction of the arrows. **If you come to a ladder**, you can either take it up to its top or pass it by (no going down ladders or hopping on or off in the middle). **If you come to a snake's head**, you *must* slide down to its tail. Can you get through this Moksha-Patamu maze to the finish?

MMM

19 TIME OUT

There are five electric clocks below, but only one of them shows the correct time. Since all of these clocks keep accurate time when they are plugged in, all you need to do is find out which one is plugged in to know which one is correct. Starting from the clocks, can you do it in less than 60 seconds? **M**

Where is the best place to buy clock parts?

At a second-hand store.

20 GEAR UP

On a trip to Luzerne, Switzerland, last year, I met a clockmaker by the name of Sven Zeitfleugen. He builds clocks that are so complicated, other Swiss clockmakers shake their heads in wonder.

I told Sven about my maze collection and asked him if he would be interested in trying to create a clock for it. The incredibly complex clock design on the next page is what Sven came up with.

Starting at the winding key in the lower left, can you find a path through the cogwheels and axles that will take you to the escape wheel in the upper right?

To solve this maze, you can travel between cogwheels that touch or between cogwheels that share an axle.

I'm wheely weady for this one.

M M

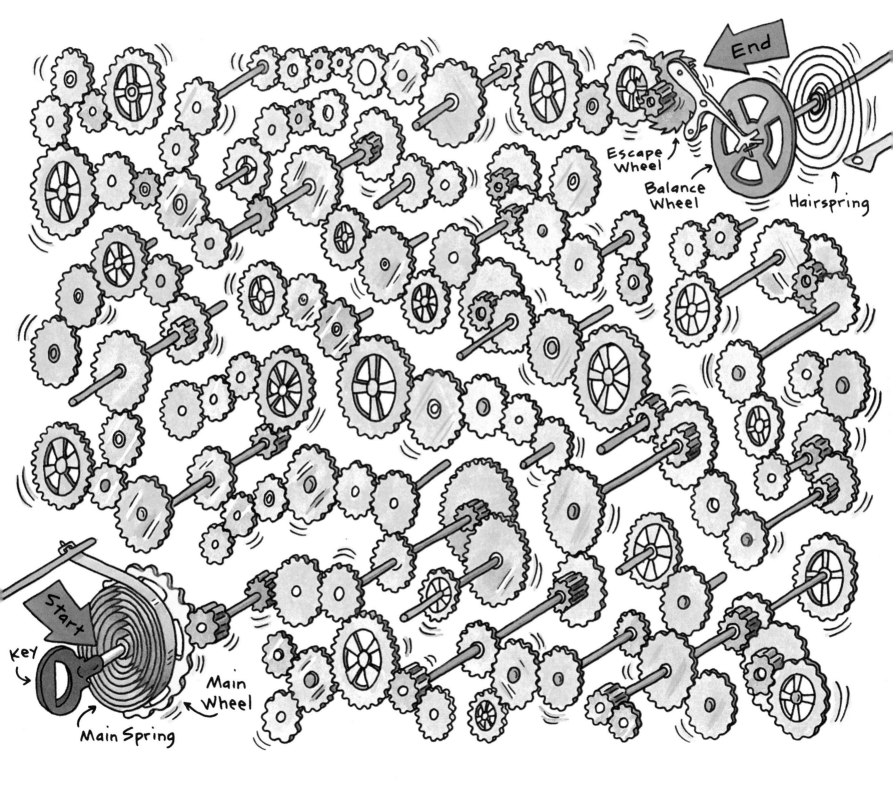

End

Escape Wheel

Balance Wheel

Hairspring

Start

Key

Main Spring

Main Wheel

21 MAP TRAP

The map below shows the area surrounding Mastermind Headquarters. Quite a mess of one-way streets, isn't it? That's the way I like it. Following the arrows, can you find a route that will take you from "Start" to the red "End" arrow? **M**

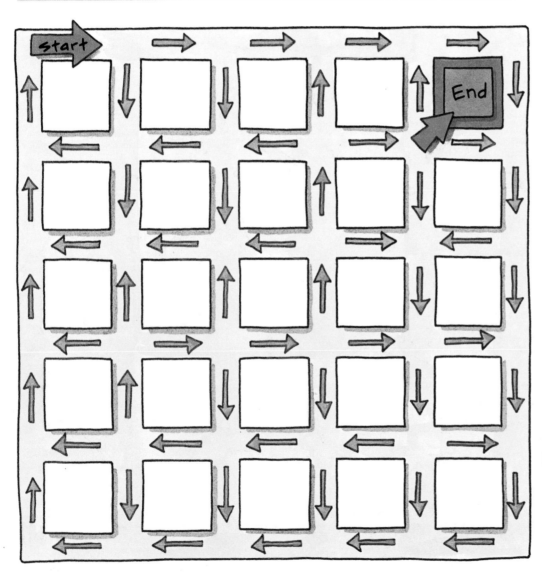

22 GLOBE TROTTING

We're almost at the end of our tour, but that doesn't mean the Mastermind challenges are over.

Posted on the next page is a map of the world. That you probably already knew. What you may not know is that there is a way to travel around this map so that you visit *every* place marked on it *exactly once*.

Starting and ending in Greece, can you figure out the correct route? Remember, you can move only in the directions indicated by the arrows, and your path must visit each country only once.

(In case you're wondering, the spots marked on this map are the places where I picked up all of the mazes in this book.)

I call it whirled world.

MM

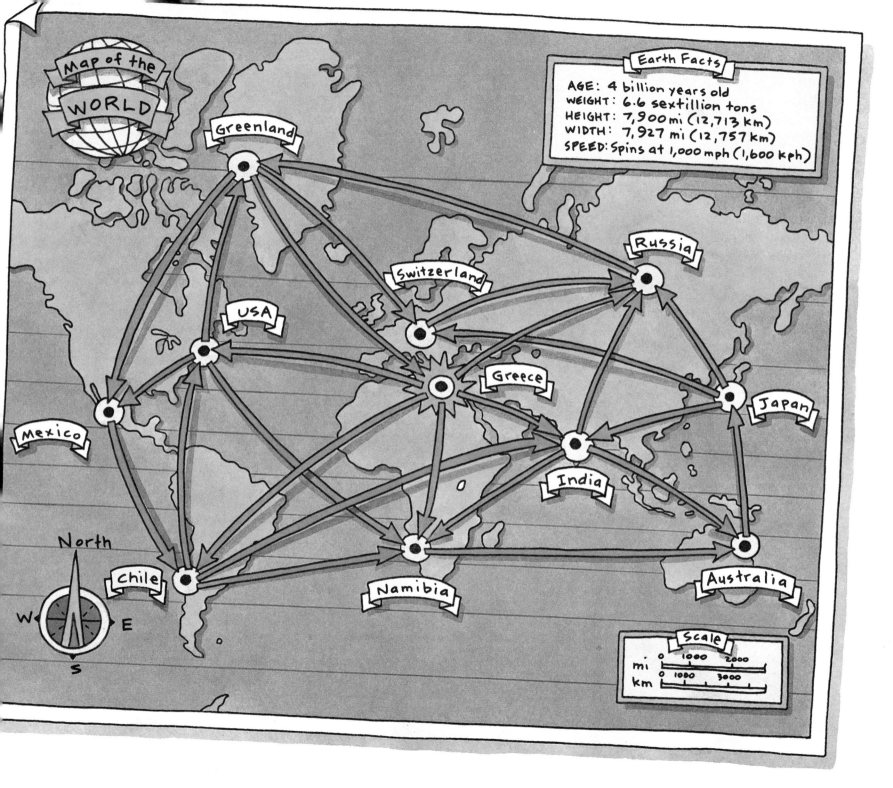

23 WAY OUT

Well, congratulations! I didn't think you could make it through our collection of trap-filled trickery. I can tell by the way your eyeballs are spinning that you must have enjoyed yourself. Before you leave, though, you're going to have to do one last bit of work.

To the right, you will see a floor plan of Mastermind Headquarters. Doesn't look like it, you say? That's because our architect forgot to fill in the walls on his drawing—he got only as far as drawing in and numbering the columns.

The first thing you have to do is finish the drawing by filling in the walls like a dot-to-dot puzzle. Once you've done that, find a way from the star on the floor plan that says "You are here" to the door marked "Exit."

Can you do it all before the Headquarters shuts down for the day? You have four minutes!

MM

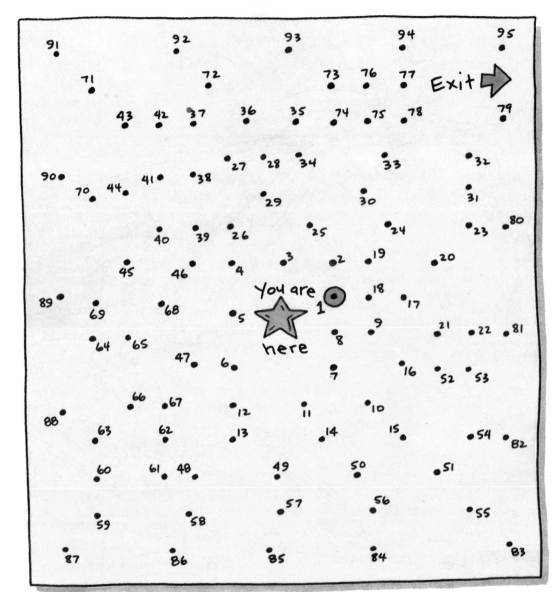

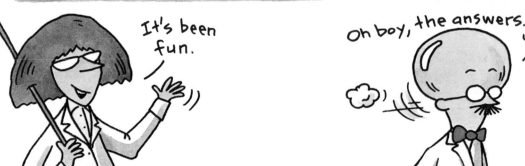

Answers

1 MAIZE MAZE

3 RAIL TRAIL

2 'TEC TREK

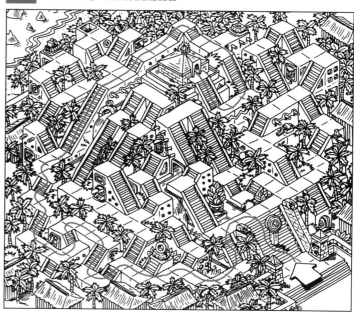

4 IN A HOLE

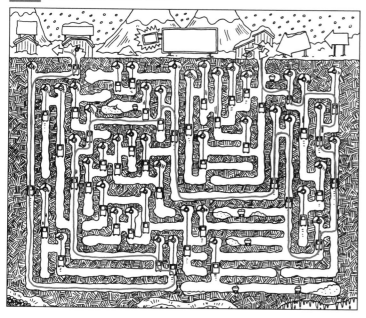

6 BOARD YET?

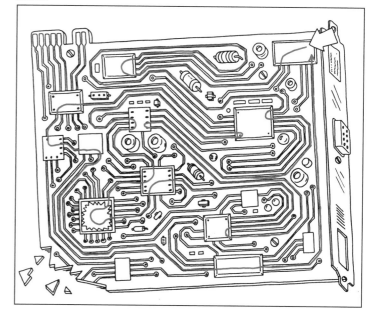

5 OF CORDS

7 IT'S ALL GREEK TO ME

8 MINOTAUR GOLF

Tee #1 leads to the hole.

10 TILT!

12 I SEE

9 GO GET 'EM

13 WATER WAY TO GO

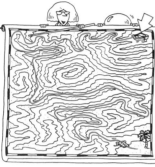

11 VINE LINE

The correct route spells "melon" (in script).

15 FOLLOW THE BOUNCING BALL

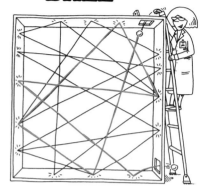

14 GOOD G-REEF

16 HAVE A BALL

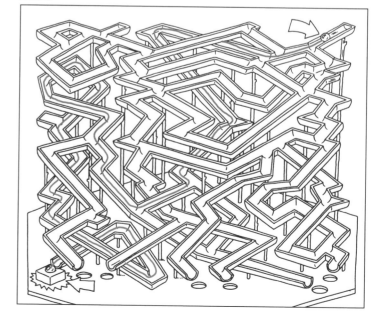

17 ROLL ON

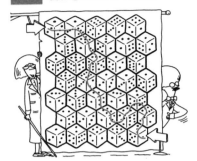

21 MAP TRAP

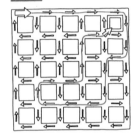

20 GEAR UP

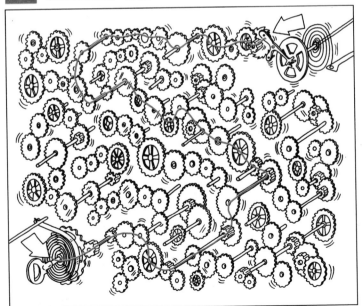

18 NO DICE

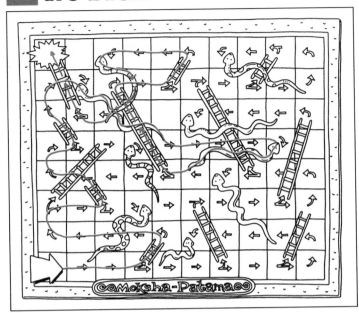

©Moksha-Patama©

19 TIME OUT

It's clock #1!

23 WAY OUT

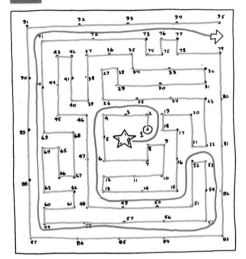

22 GLOBE TROTTING

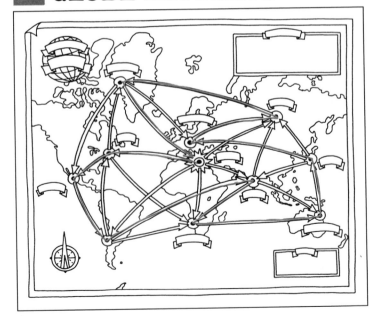